Canada

RUSSIA

Arctic Circle

60°

BERING STRAIT

BEAUFORT
SEA

U S A

Holma
Islan

YUKON

NORTHWEST

● Whitehorse

Yellowknife

PACIFIC

OCEAN

Prince Rupert

BRITISH
COLUMBIA

C

Edmonton ●

ALBERT

VANCOUVER
ISLAND

Banff ●   Calga

● Vancouver

Lethbridge

Pincher Creek ●

Victoria

75°

60°

45°

30°

15°

0°

15°

30°

45°

90° 105° 120° 135° 150° 165° 180° 165° 150° 135° 120° 105° 90° 75° 60° 45° 30° 15° 0° 15° 30° 45° 60° 75° 90°

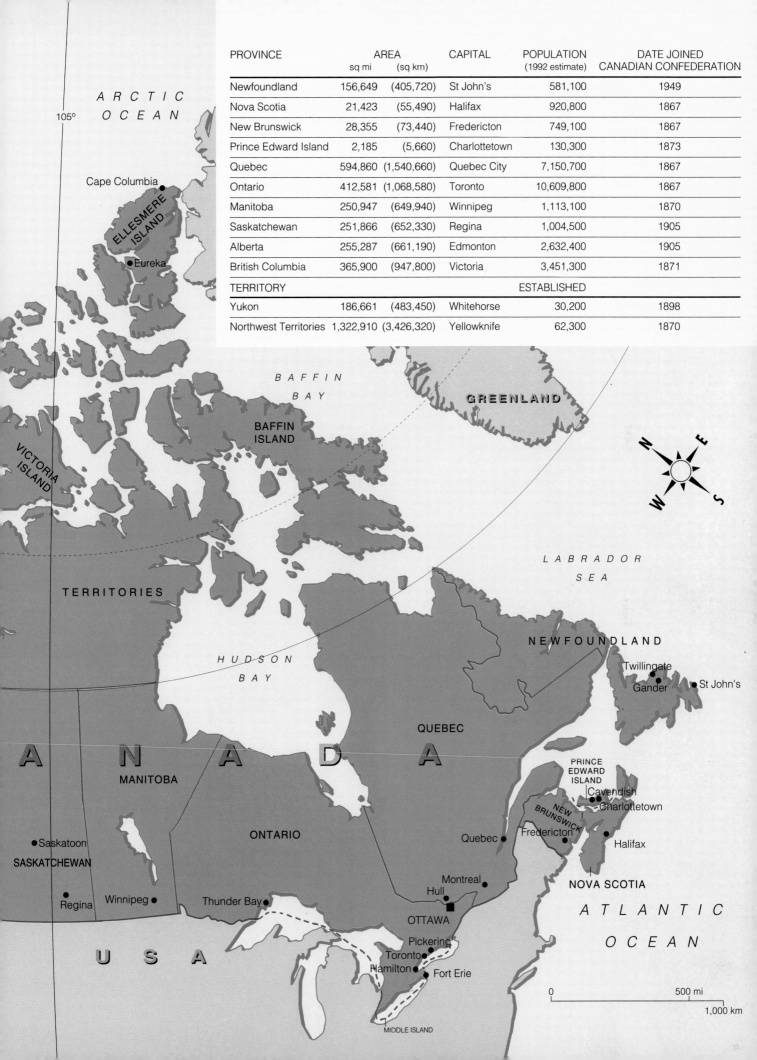

| PROVINCE | AREA | | CAPITAL | POPULATION | DATE JOINED |
	sq mi	(sq km)		(1992 estimate)	CANADIAN CONFEDERATION
Newfoundland	156,649	(405,720)	St John's	581,100	1949
Nova Scotia	21,423	(55,490)	Halifax	920,800	1867
New Brunswick	28,355	(73,440)	Fredericton	749,100	1867
Prince Edward Island	2,185	(5,660)	Charlottetown	130,300	1873
Quebec	594,860	(1,540,660)	Quebec City	7,150,700	1867
Ontario	412,581	(1,068,580)	Toronto	10,609,800	1867
Manitoba	250,947	(649,940)	Winnipeg	1,113,100	1870
Saskatchewan	251,866	(652,330)	Regina	1,004,500	1905
Alberta	255,287	(661,190)	Edmonton	2,632,400	1905
British Columbia	365,900	(947,800)	Victoria	3,451,300	1871
TERRITORY				ESTABLISHED	
Yukon	186,661	(483,450)	Whitehorse	30,200	1898
Northwest Territories	1,322,910	(3,426,320)	Yellowknife	62,300	1870

Canada

John Sylvester

RAINTREE STECK-VAUGHN
PUBLISHERS

Austin, Texas

Published by Raintree Steck-Vaughn Publishers, an imprint of
Steck-Vaughn Company

Design Roger Kohn
Editors Diana Russell, Pam Wells
DTP editor Helen Swansbourne
Picture research John Sylvester, Valerie Mulcahy
Illustration János Márffy
Commissioning editor Debbie Fox

Special thanks to Nicky Cleaveland of the
Prince Edward Island Government Services Library

Front cover: John Sylvester *above*, Roger Kohn *below*;
Bryan and Cherry Alexander, pages 17, 23, 26; First Light,
Toronto, pages 8/9 (Ken Straiton), 11 *above* (Richard Hartmier),
12 (Brian Milne), 13 *below* (Robert Semenuik), 14
(Jerry Kobalenko), 16 *above* (Grant Black) and *below*
(David Nunuk), 18 (Larry Macdougal), 19, 22 (Jessie Parker), 24
below (Dave Reede), 24/25 (Pat Morrow), 25 *below*, 28 *above*
(Tom Kitchin), 31 (Ken Straiton), 32/33, 34 (Tom Kitchin),
35 *below*, 37 (Pat Morrow), 38 (Richard Hartmier), 39 *above*
(Chris Harris), 40 *above*, 43 (Tom Kitchin); Robert Harding
Picture Library, page 35 *above*; Roger Kohn, page 21 *below*;
Reflexion, pages 21 *above* (Ives Tessier), 29 (Sheila Naimen),
30 (Michel Gascon); Tony Stone Images, pages 28 *below*, 41;
John Sylvester, pages 8, 11 *below*, 13 *above*, 15, 20, 24 *above*
left, 27, 32 *below*, 33 *below*, 39 *below*, 40 *below*, 42; Telegraph
Colour Library (Colorific), page 36

The statistics given in this book are the most up to date available
at the time of going to press

Printed and bound in Hong Kong by
Wing King Tong Co., Ltd.

1 2 3 4 5 6 7 8 9 0 PO 99 98 97 96 95

Library of Congress Cataloging-in-Publication Data
Sylvester, John, 1955–
Canada / John Sylvester.
p. cm. – (Country fact files)
Includes bibliographical references and index.
ISBN 0-8114-6197-1
1. Canada – Juvenile literature.
I. Title. II. Series.
F1008.2.S95 1996
971–dc20
95-38084
CIP AC

CONTENTS

Words that are explained in the glossary are printed in
SMALL CAPITALS the first time they are mentioned in the text.

⚜ INTRODUCTION

Canada is the second largest country in the world (after the Russian Federation). Its relatively small population of 28.7 million people live in only 11 percent of the country's area.

Canadians have exploited their country's wealth of natural resources to build one of the world's richest societies. The highly industrialized economy produces items ranging from paper and steel to communications satellites and nuclear reactors. Canada is the world's seventh largest economy, after the U.S., Japan, Germany, France, Italy, and the U.K.

As well as a high standard of living, Canadians enjoy cleaner air, lower crime rates, and better health and education than many industrialized countries. These are

▲ Toronto is Canada's largest city. Its distinctive skyline is dominated by the CN tower, the world's largest free-standing structure.

◀ Moraine Lake is just one of many lakes in the Rocky Mountains created by melting GLACIERS. This famous view was once pictured on the Can $10 bill.

some reasons why in 1994 the United Nations rated Canada the best country in the world to live in.

Canada was once a British colony. It is still a member of the Commonwealth. However, since the end of World War II, ties to Britain have steadily declined. The most important influence today is the U.S. With a population ten times larger than Canada's, its influence can be overwhelming. The two countries share the longest undefended border in the world – 5,524 miles (8,890 km). Most Canadians live less than a day's drive from the border. But they don't have to cross it to experience American culture. They just turn on their televisions. Some 64 percent of the programs they watch are from the U.S.

In the province of Quebec, 82 percent of people speak French as their first language. Their society and culture are unique, and very different from English Canada's. Many Quebecers would like to protect their culture by separating from Canada to form their own country. Finding a way for people of French and English origin to live together in harmony has always been Canada's greatest challenge.

THE LANDSCAPE

Canada stretches 3,418 miles (5,500 km) from east to west — one-quarter of the distance around the world. Its southern-most point, Middle Island in Lake Erie, shares the same latitude as the French Riviera, while the northern-most point, Cape Columbia on Ellesmere Island, is only 477 miles (768 km) from the North Pole. In between lies 2,500 miles (4,000 km) of mostly wilderness.

There are six geographical regions. The Canadian Shield is the largest, occupying nearly half of the country's area. It takes its name from the hard bedrock that underlies the region. It is noted for its many lakes and rivers, thin soil, dense forests, and abundant wildlife. Most of Lake Superior — the largest freshwater lake in the world — lies within the region.

Boreal, or northern, forest covers much of the Canadian Shield. This is a mixture of evergreen trees such as pine, spruce, fir, and cedar, and a few deciduous trees such as birch and aspen. The forest is home to beavers, moose, black bears, wolves, lynx, porcupines, and many other animals.

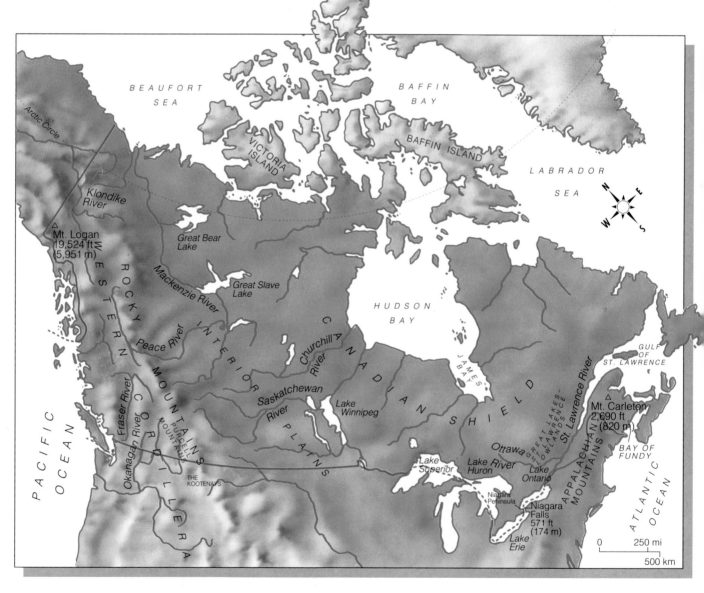

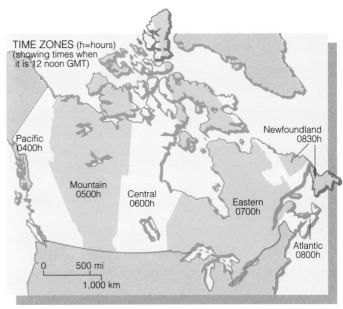

TIME ZONES (h=hours)
(showing times when
it is 12 noon GMT)

Pacific
0400h

Mountain
0500h

Central
0600h

Eastern
0700h

Newfoundland
0830h

Atlantic
0800h

0   500 mi

1,000 km

▲ *Lake Superior is the largest of the Great Lakes. Its rocky northern shore is part of the Canadian Shield.*

▼ *The spectacular Rocky Mountains were formed by movements in the Earth's surface some 60 million years ago.*

West of the Canadian Shield lies the Interior Plains. This area was ground flat during the last Ice Age. The retreating glaciers left behind rich deposits of topsoil, ideal for growing grain. Canadians call this flat, treeless region "the prairies." Early explorers named it after the French word "prairie," which means "meadow."

The Western Cordillera is a huge range of mountains that stretches along the western edge of North and South America. The Canadian portion consists of two mountain ranges, with peaks as high as 19,700 feet (6,000 m). The coastal range borders the Pacific Ocean and is covered by dense rainforest. Thousand-year-old Douglas firs grow to 295 feet (90 m) in height and 16 feet (5 m) in diameter. The eastern mountain range, the famous Rocky Mountains, face the Interior Plains. In between the two are smaller ranges and plateaus.

The Arctic region in Canada's far north consists of hundreds of islands in the Arctic Ocean. The area is dominated by TUNDRA, a treeless plain of mosses, lichens, grasses, and shrubs.

In eastern Canada, the Appalachians cover most of the four Atlantic provinces. This ancient mountain range has been worn

◀ *This prairie farmland near Winnipeg, Manitoba, is part of Canada's largest agricultural region.*

KEY FACTS

● At 2,635 miles (4,241 km), the Mackenzie is the second longest river in North America, after the Mississippi–Missouri river system.

● The world's highest tides occur in the Bay of Fundy. The bay's long, narrow shape means that the difference between high and low tides can be as much as 52 feet (16 m).

● 8% of Canada is covered by lakes and rivers, which contain 30% of the world's freshwater – enough to flood the entire country to a depth of 6.6 feet (2 m).

● Newfoundland has its own time zone, 30 minutes ahead of the Maritime Provinces (Prince Edward Island, New Brunswick, and Nova Scotia).

THE LANDSCAPE

down by glaciers to low rolling hills with fertile river valleys in between. Mount Carleton, in the province of New Brunswick, is the highest peak, at 2,858 feet (817 m). A rugged coastline of cliffs, bays, beaches, and many islands meets the Atlantic Ocean.

The smallest geographical region is the Great Lakes–St. Lawrence lowlands, a tiny area of rich agricultural land sandwiched between the Canadian Shield and the Appalachians. More than 60 percent of Canadians live here, in the urban centers of Quebec and Ontario.

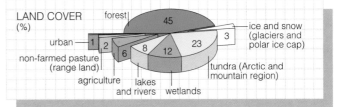

LAND COVER (%): forest 45, ice and snow (glaciers and polar ice cap) 3, tundra (Arctic and mountain region) 23, wetlands 12, lakes and rivers 8, agriculture 6, non-farmed pasture (range land) 2, urban 1

Canada has the world's longest coastline 151,490 miles (243,792 km), including 52,455 islands. Shown here is the rocky coastline near Twillingate, Newfoundland.

In the western Arctic, the Mackenzie River breaks up into many smaller channels before finally emptying into the Beaufort Sea.

13

◼ CLIMATE AND WEATHER

Canada is the coldest country in the world. Its average annual temperature is only 22°F (–5.6°C).

In the Arctic, the ground is permanently frozen. This PERMAFROST lies under more than 40 percent of the country. But the Arctic receives less snowfall than the rest of Canada. If it were not for the cold temperatures, this would be a desert. Canada's coldest weather station is at Eureka, Ellesmere Island, with an average annual temperature of –3°F (–19.7°C).

The warm Pacific Ocean means the west coast has the mildest winters. This area also has the most rain. Prince Rupert, 311 miles (500 km) north of Vancouver, has 94 inches (240 cm) of rain and snow a year.

The Cordillera Mountains stop the moist

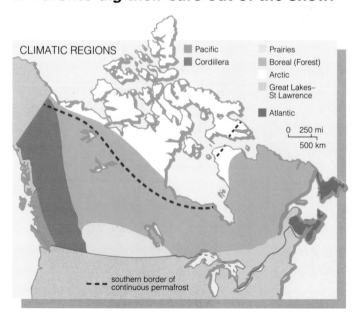

▲ *Every winter, snowstorms bring traffic to a stop in Canadian cities. Here, people in Toronto dig their cars out of the snow.*

CLIMATIC REGIONS
- Pacific
- Cordillera
- Prairies
- Boreal (Forest)
- Arctic
- Great Lakes–St Lawrence
- Atlantic

0   250 mi
500 km

- - - southern border of continuous permafrost

Pacific air from moving farther east. Winters here are cold and summers are cool. The western slopes receive as much as 236 inches (600 cm) of snow annually. This allows residents of Vancouver to play golf in the morning, then drive 62 miles (100 km) to the mountains for an afternoon of skiing.

Most of the southern prairies, on the other side of the mountains, have less than 15 inches (400 mm) of precipitation a year. Far from the moderating effects of the ocean, the prairies have an extreme (continental) climate, with cold winters and hot, dry summers. Lack of rain, combined with high temperatures and wind, can produce severe drought.

The vast Boreal (forest) region and the Great Lakes—St. Lawrence lowlands also have a continental climate, but with more precipitation. Montreal has about 93 inches (235 cm) of snow annually, more than any other major city in the world.

Atlantic Canada has some of the worst weather. Violent winter storms blow from the Atlantic Ocean, bringing heavy snow and freezing rain. St. John's, Newfoundland, is the snowiest, foggiest, wettest, windiest, and cloudiest city in Canada. It also has the most freezing rain.

KEY FACTS

● About 30% of Canada's annual precipitation falls as snow.
● The country's coldest recorded temperature was –81.4°F (–63°C) in Snag, Yukon, on February 3, 1947.
● In January 1962 in Pincher Creek, Alberta, a warm, dry wind known as a CHINOOK raised the temperature from –2°F (–19°C) to 72°F (22°C) in just 1 hour.
● A heatwave that lasted 1½ weeks struck the prairie provinces in July 1936. Temperatures reached 112°F (44.4°C) and 780 people died.

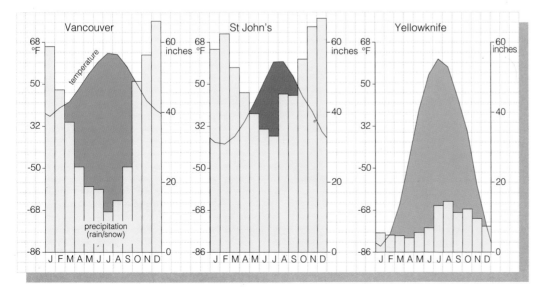

▲ *Canadians take full advantage of their short summers by gathering on beaches such as this one in Cavendish, Prince Edward Island.*

NATURAL RESOURCES

Canada has 10 percent of the world's forests, large mineral deposits, huge reserves of oil and natural gas, and many rivers used to generate hydroelectricity.

Forests cover 45 percent of the country, and half of these are commercial activities. Canada is the world's largest producer of newsprint, second largest producer of pulp (used to make newsprint), and third largest producer of lumber. Most of the industry is concentrated in British Columbia, Quebec, and Ontario, but there is some production in every province.

Canada is one of the world's largest producers of minerals. It is the world leader in zinc production (supplying 18.7% of the world's needs) and in uranium production (40% of the world's needs). It is the second largest producer of cobalt, gypsum, potash, nickel, asbestos, and titanium, and the fifth largest producer of gold. Other key metals include copper, lead, iron ore, and silver.

Most minerals are found in the hard rock

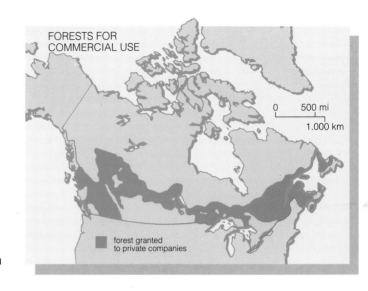

FORESTS FOR COMMERCIAL USE

0   500 mi

1.000 km

■ forest granted to private companies

▲ *Logs used for pulp and paper are surrounded by a string of logs, called a "boom," and pulled to a mill by a tugboat.*

◄ *On Vancouver Island, huge logs are loaded on trucks and taken to a sawmill.*

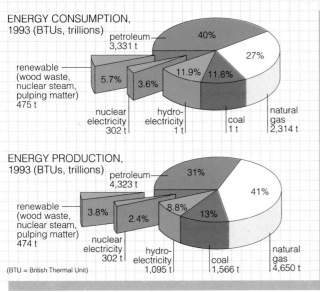

ENERGY CONSUMPTION,
1993 (BTUs, trillions)

petroleum — 3,331 t — 40%

27%

renewable
(wood waste,
nuclear steam,
pulping matter)
475 t — 5.7%

3.6%

11.9% 11.8%

nuclear
electricity
302 t

hydro-
electricity
1 t

coal
1 t

natural
gas
2,314 t

ENERGY PRODUCTION,
1993 (BTUs, trillions)

petroleum — 4,323 t — 31%

41%

renewable
(wood waste,
nuclear steam,
pulping matter)
474 t — 3.8%

2.4%

8.8% 13%

nuclear
electricity
302 t

hydro-
electricity
1,095 t

coal
1,566 t

natural
gas
4,650 t

(BTU = British Thermal Unit)

▲ *This massive dam on James Bay in
northern Quebec is part of North
America's largest hydroelectric project.
The project involves a total of 8 dams
and 198 dikes, containing 5 reservoirs.*

of the Canadian Shield. However, one-
quarter of the world's reserves of potash,
a mineral used for fertilizer, is found under
the Saskatchewan prairie. At current rates
of consumption, these reserves will last for
2,000 years.

Coal is mined in Nova Scotia, Alberta,
and British Columbia. Some of North

◀ **Oil drilling rigs are a familiar sight in Alberta. The province is Canada's leading producer of fossil fuels.**

KEY FACTS

● The James Bay project covers 4,595 sq mi (11,900 sq km) – half the size of Lake Ontario.

● Every year, forest fires, insects, and disease destroy as many trees as are harvested in Canada.

● A single train carrying the 1993 forest harvest would be 34,176 mi (55,000 km) long – 10 times the width of Canada.

● North America's largest gold rush occurred in the Yukon Territory after gold was discovered near the Klondike River in 1898.

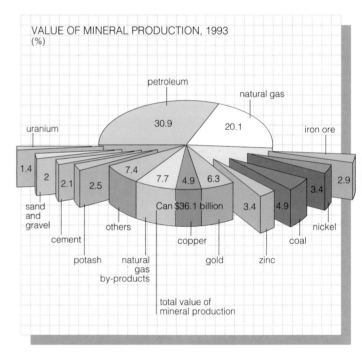

VALUE OF MINERAL PRODUCTION, 1993 (%)

petroleum 30.9
natural gas 20.1
uranium 1.4
iron ore 2.9
2
2.1
2.5
7.4
7.7
4.9
6.3
3.4
3.4
4.9
2.9
sand and gravel
cement
potash
natural gas by-products
others
copper
gold
zinc
coal
nickel
Can $36.1 billion
total value of mineral production

America's largest deposits are mined in the Kootenay region of British Columbia. Most is exported to Japan. Alberta has more than 80 percent of Canada's oil reserves. It supplies 50 percent of its oil and 90 percent of its natural gas. There are also large reserves of oil and natural gas in the Northwest Territories and off the coast of Newfoundland.

Canadian rivers generate 15 percent of the world's hydroelectric power, and two-thirds of Canada's electricity. The largest hydroelectric development is the James Bay project in northern Quebec. The combined output of its generating stations is 10,283 megawatts. The second stage of the development has been stalled by opposition from the Cree natives in the region.

POPULATION

Most Canadians live in cities, where indoor shopping MALLS are popular. This is the Eaton Center in Toronto.

THE FIRST PEOPLE

About 10,000 years ago, Stone Age hunters from Asia crossed the Bering Strait and reached North America. They were the ancestors of North America's native peoples. By the time the first Europeans arrived, more than 400 years ago, there were 350,000 native people living in what is now Canada. Much of their land was taken by white people. About 60 percent of Canada's 800,000 natives now live on RESERVES, land set aside for them by the government. Many still earn their living from traditional activities such as hunting and fishing. Others have adapted to life in white society. For example, the Mohawks have gained an international reputation for their skill as high-level construction workers building skyscrapers in New York City.

THE BRITISH AND FRENCH

Britain and France began permanent settlements in eastern Canada in the early 1600s. The two countries fought for control of the area for more than 150 years, until the French were finally defeated by the British in 1763. Most Canadians are descendants of these two groups, and today French and English are the official languages of Canada.

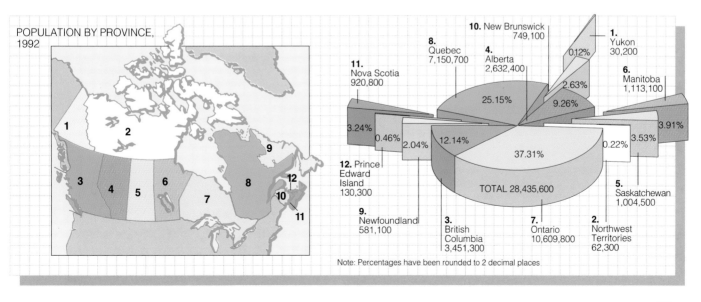

POPULATION BY PROVINCE, 1992

10. New Brunswick 749,100
8. Quebec 7,150,700
4. Alberta 2,632,400
0.12%
1. Yukon 30,200
6. Manitoba 1,113,100
11. Nova Scotia 920,800
2.63%
9.26%
25.15%
3.24%
0.46%
2.04%
12.14%
37.31%
3.91%
0.22%
3.53%
12. Prince Edward Island 130,300
TOTAL 28,435,600
5. Saskatchewan 1,004,500
9. Newfoundland 581,100
3. British Columbia 3,451,300
7. Ontario 10,609,800
2. Northwest Territories 62,300

Note: Percentages have been rounded to 2 decimal places

▲ *Prince Edward Island is the most rural Canadian province. But it also has the highest population density, because of its small size.*

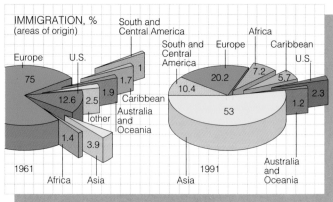

POPULATION DENSITY, 1992
(people per sq mi)

Note: Figures have been rounded to nearest whole number

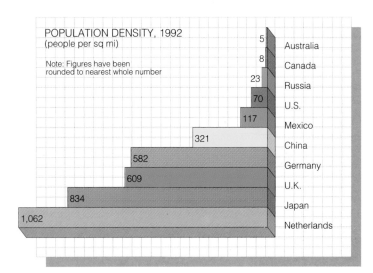

5	Australia
8	Canada
23	Russia
70	U.S.
117	Mexico
321	China
582	Germany
609	U.K.
834	Japan
1,062	Netherlands

▶ *The first Chinese immigrants came to Canada in the late 1800s. Many more have arrived in recent years, along with immigrants from other Asian countries. This Chinese-Canadian woman and her children are shopping in an East Indian area of Vancouver.*

► *In Quebec City, all street signs are in French, the language spoken by most people in the province.*

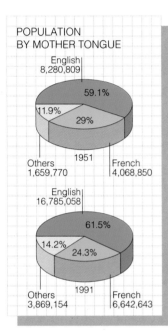

POPULATION
BY MOTHER TONGUE

English
8,280,809

59.1%

11.9%   29%

Others   French
1,659,770   4,068,850

1951

English
16,785,058

61.5%

14.2%   24.3%

Others   French
3,869,154   6,642,643

1991

The majority of French-speakers live in Quebec. However, there are small groups in almost every province. In New Brunswick, Nova Scotia, and Prince Edward Island the French are called Acadians, after "Arcadie," a name given to the region by an early French explorer.

The Northwest Territories are the only part of the country where most people are neither French nor English. More than 70 percent are Native Americans.

IMMIGRATION

When Canada was founded in 1867, its population was 3.4 million. By 1993, it was estimated at 29 million people. Most of this population growth was due to immigration. Between 1901 and 1981, Canada accepted a total of more than 8 million immigrants.

During the early 1900s the government attracted settlers to western Canada by offering them cheap farmland. When there was mass unemployment across the world in the 1930s, more people left Canada than entered. However, immigration picked up again after the World War II when Canada's growing economy needed skilled workers.

Until the 1960s, the majority of immigrants came from Britain and Europe. Today, most come from Asia. Some are refugees fleeing political oppression and war in their own countries. Others are seeking new business opportunities. Most settle in cities. Vancouver, for example, is home to many people from Hong Kong who left the British colony to avoid living under Chinese rule. Hong Kong will become part of China in 1997.

KEY FACTS

● The population in 1867 (3.4 million) was less than that of Toronto today.
● The Northwest Territories cover more than a third of Canada's area but contain less than 1% of its population.
● 80% of Canadians live within 199 miles (320 km) of the U.S. border.
● Fifty-three native languages are still spoken in Canada. The most widely known are Cree, Ojibwa, and Inuktitut.

CITIES

In 1851, when Canada was still a British colony, only 13 percent of people lived in cities. The proportion of city-dwellers has increased steadily. Now three-quarters of Canadians live in cities. Ontario is the most urbanized province — about 83 percent of the population live in a town or city. British Columbia and Alberta are next, with about 79 percent. Prince Edward Island is the least urban province, with two-thirds of its residents living in rural areas.

◄ *These children are taking part in a* POWWOW *at the Six Nations Reserve in Ontario. The festival of traditional music and dance is a popular way for native people to celebrate their culture.*

DAILY LIFE

Canadians enjoy a very high standard of living. The average family income in 1991 was about Can $53,000, compared with Can $41,000 in the U.S. Six out of ten families live in single-family homes, usually in the suburbs. Families are small — 1.8 children per couple — and in 60 percent of households, both parents work.

EDUCATION

Some 89 percent of Canadians between the ages of six and 23 attend school, college, or university. This is the highest rate in the world. In the U.S. the figure is 86 percent; in Britain it is 72 percent. The world average is 49 percent.

School is compulsory until the age of 16.

▲ *When Ottawa's Rideau Canal freezes over in winter, it becomes the world's longest skating rink and a popular spot for the city's residents.*

It begins with kindergarten, then elementary school, junior high, and high school. Most children attend publicly funded schools, but there are private schools too. After high school, at the age of 18, students with sufficiently high marks may attend one of Canada's 69 universities or 203 colleges.

The school year begins in September and ends in June. There are short breaks at Christmas and in March, with summer vacations in July and August. In some

▼ *The snowmobile was invented by a Canadian in 1937. Snowmobiling is now one of the fastest-growing winter pastimes in the country.*

farming regions, such as northern New Brunswick, students have a week off in the autumn to help with the harvesting of crops.

French immersion programs provide special instruction in French. These programs help students become deeply involved in learning the new language. Today some 300,000 students are involved.

LEISURE

Canada's long winters mean sports, such as skiing, skating, and ice hockey are popular. Ice hockey, invented in Montreal in 1885, is often called "Canada's game." Most of the players in the National Hockey League are Canadian, even though most teams are located in the U.S. Baseball and football are also popular team sports.

▼ *Canadian children often learn to play ice hockey on outdoor rinks like this one. Many dream of one day playing in the National Hockey League.*

KEY FACTS

- There are 64 televisions for every 100 people in Canada (compared with 81 in the U.S. and 43 in the U.K.), and 78 telephones per 100 people (79 in the U.S. and 46 in the U.K.).
- In 1992, the Toronto Blue Jays baseball team won the World Series – the first team outside the U.S. ever to do so. They won the series again in 1993.
- Lacrosse is the oldest organized sport in North America. It was originally a native game called "baggatway".
- Alcoholism among the native population is 13 times that of white Canadians, and their life expectancy is 10 years less than the Canadian average of 77 years.

▼ *Swimmers enjoy the wave pool at the world's largest indoor mall in Edmonton, Alberta.*

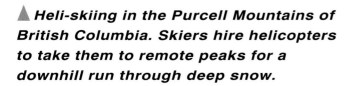

▲ *Heli-skiing in the Purcell Mountains of British Columbia. Skiers hire helicopters to take them to remote peaks for a downhill run through deep snow.*

RELIGIOUS DAYS AND HOLIDAYS

January 1	NEW YEAR'S DAY
March or April	EASTER
3rd Monday in May	VICTORIA DAY (Queen Victoria's birthday)
June 24	SAINT-JEAN BAPTISTE DAY (Quebec only)
July 1	CANADA DAY
1st Monday in August	CIVIC DAY (in most provinces)
1st Monday in September	LABOR DAY
2nd Monday in October	THANKSGIVING DAY
November 11	REMEMBRANCE DAY
December 25	CHRISTMAS DAY
December 26	BOXING DAY

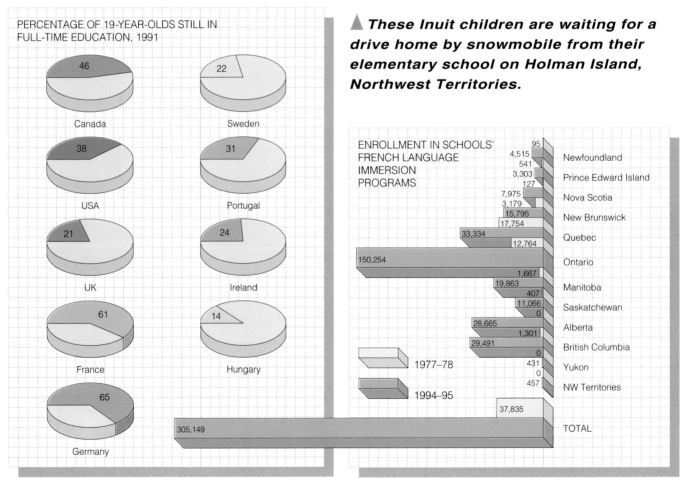

PERCENTAGE OF 19-YEAR-OLDS STILL IN FULL-TIME EDUCATION, 1991

46 Canada	22 Sweden
38 USA	31 Portugal
21 UK	24 Ireland
61 France	14 Hungary
65 Germany	

These Inuit children are waiting for a drive home by snowmobile from their elementary school on Holman Island, Northwest Territories.

ENROLLMENT IN SCHOOLS' FRENCH LANGUAGE IMMERSION PROGRAMS

	1977–78	1994–95
Newfoundland	95	4,515
Prince Edward Island	541	3,303
Nova Scotia	127	7,975
New Brunswick	3,179	15,795
Quebec	17,754	33,334
Ontario	12,764	150,254
Manitoba	1,667	19,863
Saskatchewan	407	11,066
Alberta	0	28,665
British Columbia	1,301	29,491
Yukon	0	431
NW Territories	0	457
TOTAL	37,835	305,149

▲ *Picnics are a popular way for many Canadian families to enjoy their brief summers. This family's picnic includes lobster, an Atlantic provinces delicacy.*

Canadians make the best use of their short summers. Many have summer homes near lakes or at the shore. Others go camping and hiking in wilderness areas.

SOCIAL PROBLEMS
Government-funded social programs include health care, unemployment insurance, and old age pensions. However, some people still suffer the effects of poverty. Natives are the poorest. More than 60 percent receive some kind of government aid.

RELIGION
Most Canadians are Christians. About 46 percent are Roman Catholic and 36 percent are Protestant. Another 12.4 percent say they have no religion at all. There are also small groups of Jewish people and of Moslems, Hindus, Buddhists, and Sikhs.

Most native people were converted to Christianity by white missionaries, and in some parts of the country their old religious practices were banned. But many are now returning to their traditional beliefs.

RULES AND LAWS

In 1867 the British Parliament passed the British North America (BNA) Act, uniting the colonies of Upper and Lower Canada (now Ontario and Quebec) with New Brunswick and Nova Scotia. Canadians call this event Confederation. The six other provinces joined the country later. Newfoundland was the last, in 1949.

The BNA Act did not give Canada independence. For example, it could not make its own foreign policy. In 1931, Britain passed the Statute of Westminster, recognizing Canada's independence, but the British Parliament still had to approve any changes to the constitution. In 1982,

▲ *The Royal Canadian Mounted Police is Canada's national police force. This Mountie wears the famous red jacket as part of his dress uniform.*

◄ *Ottawa's Parliament buildings are home to the national government. The changing of the guard is a daily tourist attraction in the summer.*

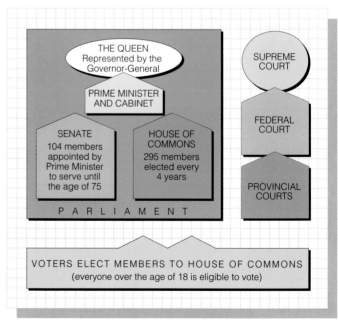

THE QUEEN
Represented by the Governor-General

PRIME MINISTER AND CABINET

SENATE
104 members appointed by Prime Minister to serve until the age of 75

HOUSE OF COMMONS
295 members elected every 4 years

PARLIAMENT

SUPREME COURT

FEDERAL COURT

PROVINCIAL COURTS

VOTERS ELECT MEMBERS TO HOUSE OF COMMONS
(everyone over the age of 18 is eligible to vote)

the Constitution Act replaced the BNA Act and Canadians finally gained control of their own affairs.

Canada is a member of the British Commonwealth, and the queen of England is the Canadian monarch. The governor-general, whose role is mainly ceremonial, is the queen's representative in Canada.

The national, or federal, government controls areas such as transportation, defense, immigration, finance, postal services, banking, and native affairs. Laws are made by the 295 elected members of the House of Commons. Five parties are currently represented in Parliament: the Liberals, the Progressive Conservatives, the New Democratic Party, the Bloc Quebecois, and the Reform Party. The Senate, made up of 104 members appointed by the prime minister, must also approve laws.

Each province has its own government which controls education, health care, local governments, social welfare, language, and culture. In 1976, the people of Quebec elected the Parti Quebecois, which wants

the province to become an independent country. In 1980, a referendum on this was held in Quebec, but it was defeated. In November 1995 Quebec held another referendum for separation, which was very narrowly defeated. Canada today is still one country.

▶ **Demonstrators in Montreal wave the Quebec flag and carry placards in favor of an independent Quebec.**

FOOD AND FARMING

Canadians generally eat a Western diet. A typical suppertime meal consists of meat (beef, pork, or poultry), potatoes or rice, and a vegetable. Residents of the Atlantic provinces and British Columbia tend to eat more seafood. In Quebec, dishes such as tourtière (a meat pie) and sugar pie (made with brown sugar and maple syrup) are eaten on special occasions. Eating out is popular everywhere, especially at fast-food restaurants such as McDonald's.

There are 111.2 million acres (45 million ha) of farmland in Canada, more than twice the area of Great Britain. Agricultural products account for 10 percent of the Canadian economy and more than half of them are exported.

The prairie provinces of Alberta, Saskatchewan, and Manitoba contain 82 percent of all Canada's farmland.

Saskatchewan produces more than half the country's wheat crop, together with large quantities of other grains and oil seeds such as barley and rapeseed (used in the manufacture of margarine and vegetable oils). Alberta is Canada's main producer of beef cattle, and also of grains such as barley, oats, and wheat used in animal feed. Manitoba has more mixed farming, where crops and animals are raised on the same farm.

Ontario has the largest agricultural sector of all the provinces. Livestock farmers there raise dairy and beef cattle, pigs, and poultry. Corn, soybeans, grains, and forage (grasses used for cattle feed) are the chief crops. Most of Canada's fruits are grown in the Niagara Peninsula.

More than half the farms in Quebec are dairy farms. This province is also the

KEY FACTS

● Canada supplies about 16% of the world's wheat.
● If the entire 1993 grain crop were loaded on a single train, it would be 13,670 mi (22,000 km) long – 4 times the width of Canada.
● The world's largest wheat field was sown near Lethbridge, Alberta, in 1951. It covered more than 34,594 acres (14,000 ha).
● In 1976, Canadians ate a record 180 pounds (82 kg) of red meat per person. That is about 360 hamburgers and 360 pork chops each! By 1991, this had fallen to 149 pounds (68 kg) per person.
● Canadians spend about 10% of their disposable incomes (earnings after tax) on food, one of the lowest proportions in industrialized countries.

▲ **Peaches and other fruits being sold at a roadside market on the Niagara Peninsula in Ontario. It is Canada's largest fruit-growing area.**

◄ **These children are eating maple candy, which is made by pouring boiling maple syrup onto snow. School tours of maple trees are very popular in Quebec and Ontario.**

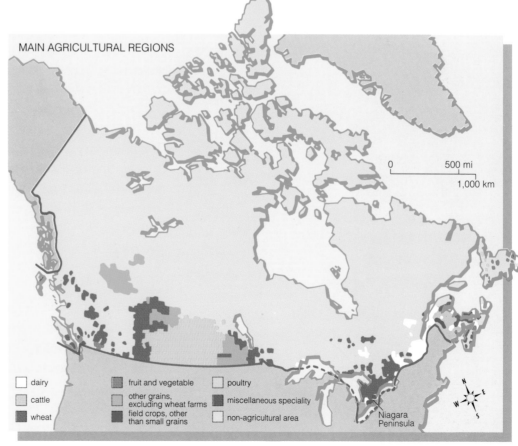

MAIN AGRICULTURAL REGIONS

0 500 mi
1,000 km

☐ dairy

☐ cattle

■ wheat

■ fruit and vegetable

☐ other grains, excluding wheat farms

■ field crops, other than small grains

☐ poultry

■ miscellaneous speciality

☐ non-agricultural area

Niagara Peninsula

world's largest producer of maple syrup, which is made by boiling down the sap collected from maple trees. It is delicious eaten on pancakes.

In the Maritime provinces, small mixed farms are most common. Nova Scotia is famous for its apples and blueberries, while Prince Edward Island is the country's largest potato producer. New Brunswick produces potatoes, livestock, and apples.

Only 2 percent of British Columbia is suitable for farming. Most are dairy and livestock farms located in the fertile Fraser River Valley. There is also a fruit-growing area in the Okanagan Valley in south-central British Columbia, where apples, peaches, plums, apricots, and grapes are produced.

Most of the northern territories and Newfoundland are unsuitable for agriculture.

Canada is one of the world's largest exporters of fish products. But the future for

◀ *These women work in a lobster canning plant. The lobster fishery is one of the few remaining viable fisheries in Atlantic Canada.*

the industry does not look good. In 1992, the entire commercial cod fishery on the Atlantic coast was closed because of depleted fish stocks. More than 50,000 fishers and plant employees were out of work. But fishing for other species, such as lobster, scallops, crab, and herring, continues.

British Columbia's fishery is the largest in Canada, worth more than Can $550 million annually. Salmon is the most important species. However, during the past few years catches have declined, and many people fear that this fishery may also have to be closed in the future.

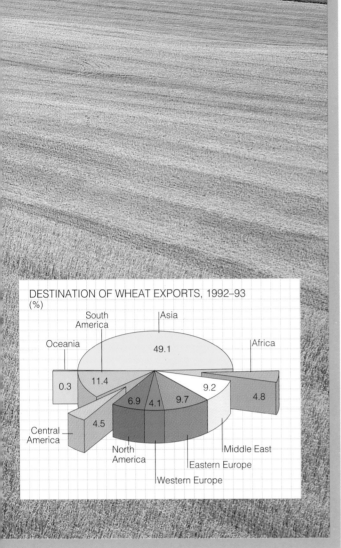

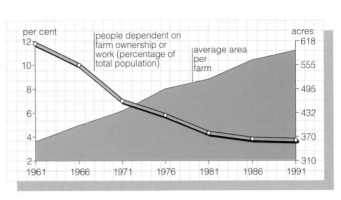

per cent — people dependent on farm ownership or work (percentage of total population) — average area per farm — acres

DESTINATION OF WHEAT EXPORTS, 1992–93
(%)

Oceania 0.3

South America 11.4

Asia 49.1

Africa 9.2

4.8

Central America 4.5

North America 6.9

4.1

9.7

Middle East

Eastern Europe

Western Europe

▼ *A huge combine harvesting grain on the prairie near Lethbridge, Alberta. Canadian farmers harvest about 30 million tons of wheat a year. Most of it is exported to Europe, Japan, China, and the Russian Federation.*

▼ *After the Netherlands, Prince Edward Island is the world's second largest exporter of seed potatoes. These are used for planting, rather than eating.*

TRADE

More than 25 percent of Canada's goods and services are sold abroad, chiefly to the U.S., which takes 75 percent of exports and provides 75 percent of imports. A free-trade agreement allows goods to pass without taxes or tariffs across the border. In 1993, the two countries signed the North America Free Trade Agreement with Mexico, creating the world's largest free-trade zone. It comes into full effect by 2003.

Canada's second largest trading partner is Japan, followed by the United Kingdom, Germany, France, and South Korea.

Natural resources such as wheat, minerals, and forestry products earned most of Canada's export income until very recently. Over 50 percent now comes from manufactured goods and services.

MANUFACTURING

Three-quarters of manufacturers are in central Canada. Ontario has more than 50 percent. Motor vehicles are the most important product. The 1965 Canada–United States Auto Pact agreement permits duty-free movement of vehicles and parts across the border. It also states that for every vehicle sold in Canada, one must be made there. This has helped Canada become the world's third largest exporter of motor vehicles, after Japan and Germany. Ontario also manufactures transportation equipment (railroad cars), chemicals, electronic products, metals like steel, and food products.

Quebec accounts for 25 percent of Canada's manufacturing industries. Paper, food processing, and textiles are the most important. The only other provinces with significant manufacturing are Alberta and British Columbia, with about 15 percent.

SERVICE INDUSTRIES

About 80 percent of all Canadian jobs are in service industries like tourism, banking, film production, restaurants, and computers.

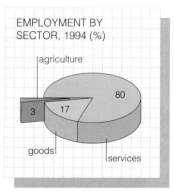

◀ *This mill on Vancouver Island produces pulp, which is used to make paper. Pulp exports are worth over Can $4 billion a year.*

EMPLOYMENT BY SECTOR, 1994 (%)

agriculture
80
3   17
goods
services

KEY FACTS

● Canada launched the world's first domestic communications satellite, the Anik A-1, in 1972.

● Canada has 177 scientists and technicians per 1,000 people – 8 times the world average. Sweden is the world leader, with 262, while the U.S. has only 55.

● The Canadian workforce totaled 13.8 million people in 1992. Women make up 45 percent of the total.

● The Candu nuclear generating station in Pickering, Ontario, is the largest producer of commercial nuclear power in the world.

● In 1939 a Czech immigrant, Thomas J. Bata, founded Bata Shoes. It is now the largest shoe-making company in the world, selling 300 million pairs in 115 countries each year.

▲ *Vancouver is Canada's busiest port. Here railroad containers carrying grain and other freight wait to be loaded onto ships.*

▶ *Motor-vehicle production is Canada's chief manufacturing industry. These vehicles are made by General Motors, the largest manufacturer.*

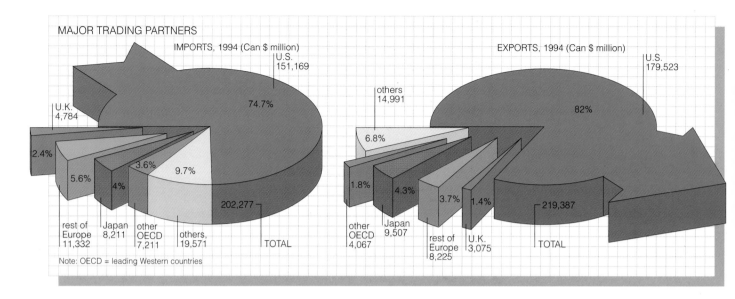

MAJOR TRADING PARTNERS

IMPORTS, 1994 (Can $ million)

U.S.
151,169

74.7%

U.K.
4,784

2.4%

5.6%

4%

3.6%

9.7%

202,277

rest of
Europe
11,332

Japan
8,211

other
OECD
7,211

others,
19,571

TOTAL

Note: OECD = leading Western countries

EXPORTS, 1994 (Can $ million)

U.S.
179,523

others
14,991

82%

6.8%

1.8%

4.3%

3.7%

1.4%

219,387

other
OECD
4,067

Japan
9,507

rest of
Europe
8,225

U.K.
3,075

TOTAL

In 1991, tourism contributed Can $25 billion to the economy and provided 554,000 jobs. Two-thirds of this revenue came from Canadians themselves, with almost Can $8 billion spent by foreign visitors. Americans are the largest group, but a growing number of tourists come from Asia.

THE WORKFORCE

Canadians are among the most skilled and highly paid workers in the world. But unemployment is high. In 1992, 1.5 million people were unemployed, or 11.2 percent of the workforce, one of the highest rates in the industrialized world. The rate was 7.3 percent in the U.S., 9.9 percent in the U.K., 4.8 percent in Germany, and 2.2 percent in Japan. One reason for this is the seasonal economy. Many workers in resource industries, or in areas such as tourism, are unemployed for part of the year.

◀ *Tourism is a major industry. These people are dogsledding in Quebec.*

▶ *Coverage of the 1988 Calgary Winter Olympics was sent around the globe by satellite dishes and satellites. Canada is a world leader in communications technology.*

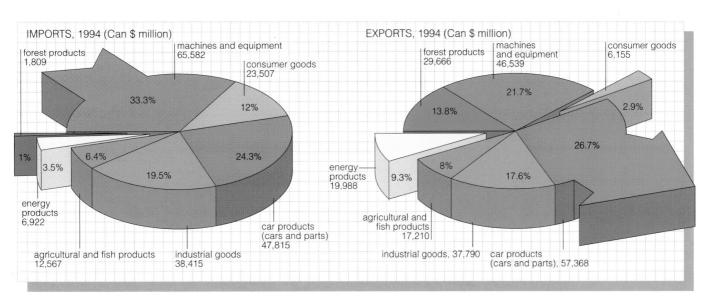

IMPORTS, 1994 (Can $ million)

forest products
1,809

machines and equipment
65,582

consumer goods
23,507

33.3%

12%

1%

3.5%

6.4%

19.5%

24.3%

energy products
6,922

agricultural and fish products
12,567

industrial goods
38,415

car products
(cars and parts)
47,815

EXPORTS, 1994 (Can $ million)

forest products
29,666

machines
and equipment
46,539

consumer goods
6,155

21.7%

13.8%

2.9%

26.7%

energy products
19,988

9.3%

8%

17.6%

agricultural and
fish products
17,210

industrial goods, 37,790

car products
(cars and parts), 57,368

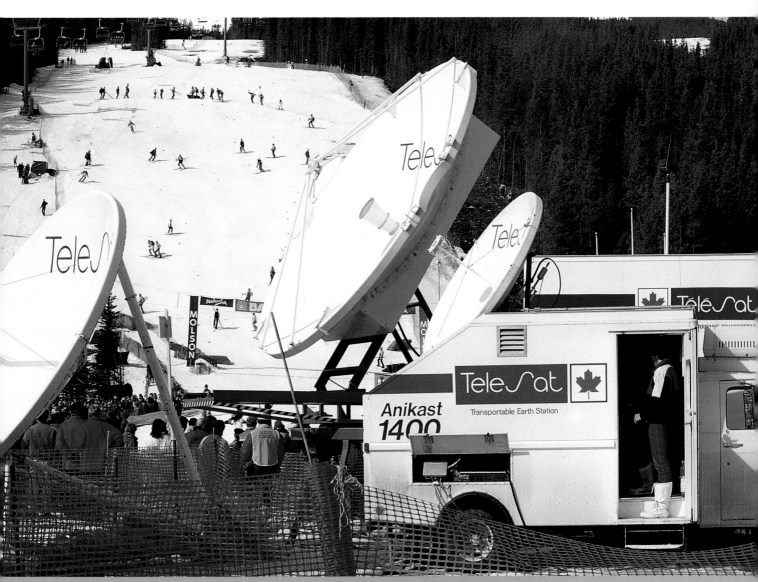

Native people and European fur traders were the first to use Canada's lakes and rivers as highways. Today, huge oceangoing ships travel almost 2,500 miles (4,000 km) from the Atlantic Ocean to the middle of the country on the St. Lawrence Seaway. Then these ships carry grain, coal, iron ore, and steel products out to markets around the world. The Seaway is operated jointly by Canada and the U.S.

Passenger ferries provide a vital link for people in isolated coastal communities along the east coast. Ferries are also important to coastal communities in British Columbia and the north.

The country's first transcontinental railroad was completed in 1885. By 1917 Canada had more miles (km) of railroad per person than any other country in the world. Prairie farmers still rely on trains to carry their grain to ports on the Great Lakes and British Columbia, where it is loaded onto ships for export. However, since the 1950s the railroads have been in decline. Cars, trucks, and airplanes have taken over.

This plane uses skis to land on Seward glacier in Kluane National Park, Yukon Territory.

Air Canada and Canadian Airlines International are the two main airlines that fly between larger cities and to U.S. and overseas destinations. More than 800 others serve the rest of the country.

Owning a car is considered a necessity for most Canadians. More than 17 million vehicles are registered in the country. Some 13 million are passenger cars. That means, there are more cars than households.

MOTOR VEHICLES PER
100 PEOPLE, 1989–90

11	Mexico
17	Poland
37	Spain
41	Germany
41	U.K.
45	Japan
49	Sweden
54	Australia
60	Canada
74	U.S.

Icebreaking ferries are the only surface transportation link in winter for the island provinces of Prince Edward Island and Newfoundland.

KEY FACTS

● The Trans-Canada Highway is the longest national highway in the world. From St John's, Newfoundland, to Victoria, British Columbia, it covers 4,860 miles (7,821 km).

● Lester B. Pearson international airport, near Toronto, is the country's busiest, handling more than 20 million passengers a year.

● Canadians drive their cars an average of 10,800 miles (17,380 km) a year, the equivalent of driving 2.7 times across the country.

▶ *This train is carrying sulfur (used in fertilizer production) and wood chips from the interior of British Columbia to ports on the coast.*

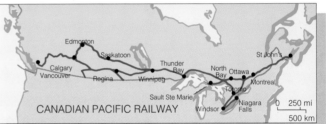

CANADIAN PACIFIC RAILWAY

0   250 mi
500 km

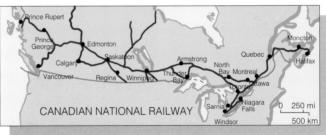

CANADIAN NATIONAL RAILWAY

0   250 mi
500 km

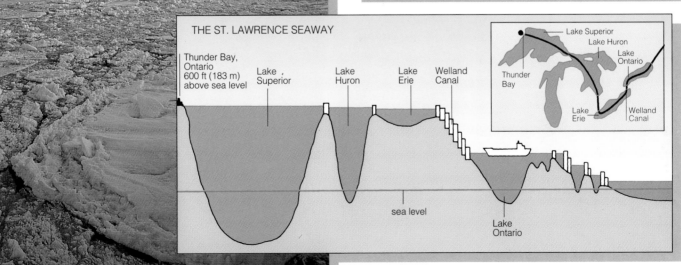

THE ST. LAWRENCE SEAWAY

Thunder Bay, Ontario 600 ft (183 m) above sea level

Lake Superior

Lake Huron

Lake Erie

Welland Canal

Thunder Bay

Lake Superior

Lake Huron

Lake Ontario

Lake Erie

Welland Canal

sea level

Lake Ontario

THE ENVIRONMENT

Most Canadians live in cities, drive cars, and buy lots of consumer goods. The result is air pollution and household waste. Canada produces more rubbish per person than any other country, 4 pounds (1.8 kg) a day. Landfill sites around urban areas are filling up, and it is becoming more expensive to dispose of solid waste. Many towns and cities now have recycling programs.

Air pollution actually decreased during the early 1990s, because of tougher motor vehicle emission standards and a ban on leaded gasoline. Acid rain, which killed lakes and damaged forests in eastern Canada during the 1970s and 1980s, has been dramatically reduced. Sulfur dioxide emissions, which cause acid rain, were cut by 50 percent in the first half of the 1990s.

Canadians are fortunate to live in a country with so much wilderness. However, only 7 percent of the total area is protected. The goal is 12 percent. Valuable areas have already been lost. For example, most of

▲ *This protest camp was set up by environmentalists to stop* CLEAR-CUTTING *on Vancouver Island. Most of British Columbia's old-growth forests have already gone.*

▼ *Gros Morne National Park in Newfoundland is one of 10 World Heritage Sites in Canada, named by the United Nations.*

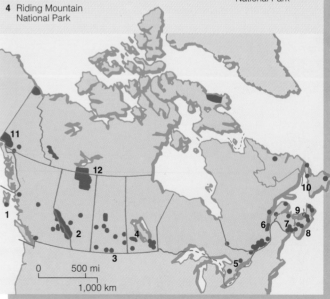

MAJOR NATIONAL PARKS

1 South Moresby/ Gwaii Haanas National Park Reserve
2 Banff National Park/Jasper National Park
3 Grasslands National Park
4 Riding Mountain National Park
5 Point Pelee National Park
6 La Mauricie National Park
7 Fundy National Park
8 Kejimkujik National Park
9 Prince Edward Island National Park
10 Gros Morne National Park
11 Kluane National Park
12 Wood Buffalo National Park

0   500 mi
1,000 km

KEY FACTS

● Wood Buffalo is Canada's largest national park. At 17,000 square miles (44,000 sq km), it is larger than Switzerland.

● 50% of the acid rain that falls in eastern Canada comes from the U.S.

● More than 20 million people visit Canada's national parks every year.

● Greenpeace originated in Vancouver in 1970 as a small group opposed to nuclear testing in the Pacific Ocean. It is now one of the best-known environmental groups in the world.

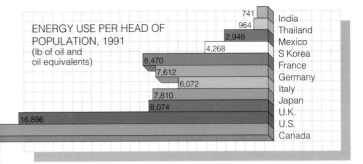

ENERGY USE PER HEAD OF POPULATION, 1991 (lb of oil and oil equivalents)

India	741
Thailand	964
Mexico	2,948
S Korea	4,268
France	8,470
Germany	7,612
Italy	6,072
Japan	7,810
U.K.	8,074
U.S.	16,896
Canada	20,658

British Columbia's old-growth forests have been cut down. Environmental groups are fighting to save the remaining areas.

Agricultural expansion on the prairies and in the Great Lakes—St. Lawrence region has also destroyed 70 percent of wetlands. Wetlands act as "sponges," absorbing excess water to protect the surrounding land from flooding. They are also important breeding grounds for tens of thousands of waterfowl, whose numbers have seriously declined since the 1970s.

As well as national wildlife areas and bird sanctuaries, Canada has 36 national parks, covering more than 77,200 square miles (200,000 sq km) — about 2 percent of the country's area. The first was set up in the Rocky Mountains near Banff, Alberta, in 1885. Banff is still the most popular park in the country, with nearly 4 million visitors a year.

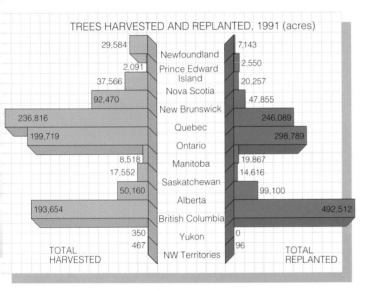

TREES HARVESTED AND REPLANTED, 1991 (acres)

TOTAL HARVESTED	Province	TOTAL REPLANTED
29,584	Newfoundland	7,143
2,091	Prince Edward Island	2,550
37,566	Nova Scotia	20,257
92,470	New Brunswick	47,855
236,816	Quebec	246,089
199,719	Ontario	298,789
8,518	Manitoba	19,867
17,552	Saskatchewan	14,616
50,160	Alberta	99,100
193,654	British Columbia	492,512
350	Yukon	0
467	NW Territories	96

◀ *Canada's huge areas of wilderness cannot escape the effects of global pollution. Toxic chemicals have even been found in the Arctic, in animals such as these polar bears.*

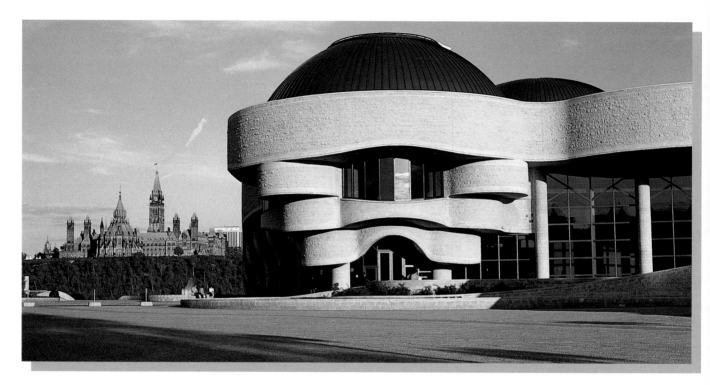

anada has a bright future. It has a wealth of natural resources and a highly skilled workforce. For 50 years it has had one of the fastest growing economies in the industrialized world. Its economy is expected to continue growing rapidly throughout the 1990s.

However, one problem the country must solve in order to secure its economic future is its debt. During the 1960s, 1970s, and 1980s, the government spent more than it collected in taxes. It borrowed money to make up the difference. Today, Canada has the highest debt per person of all the industrialized nations. In order to pay back the money it owes, the government is reducing its spending. Many Canadians are worried that they will soon have to pay more for health care and other government programs that used to be funded out of taxes alone.

Historically, Canada's biggest problem has been the conflict between its English and French communities. For example, the

▲ *The Canadian Museum of Civilization in Hull, Quebec, was designed by Douglas Cardinal, who draws on his native heritage to design curved buildings that blend into the landscape.*

▶ *Canada's fate is tied to that of its powerful neighbor, the U.S. This border crossing between Fort Erie, Ontario, and Buffalo, New York, is one of the busiest.*

referendum of 1995 showed that 49.5 percent of Quebec's population believed their province would be better off as an independent country.

Canada's native people are also trying to gain more control over their affairs. They want greater self-government and control of their traditional lands. For example, the Cree of northern Quebec are fighting the expansion of a huge hydroelectric project on their land near James Bay, which will destroy their traditional way of life. The

KEY FACTS

● Canada's government debt is set to double from Can $630 billion in 1993 to Can $1.26 trillion in 2003.

● In 1991, 11.6% of Canadians were aged 65 or more. By 2031, the proportion is expected to grow to 22%.

● On April 1, 1999, a new northern territory called "Nunavut" will be established. It will be created from central and eastern parts of the present Northwest Territories.

● The magnetic north pole, located in the Canadian Arctic, moves by up to 50 miles (80 km) a day. In 100 years' time, it may be on the Russian Federation side of the Arctic Ocean.

Cree hope to stop this expansion by joining forces with international environmental groups.

Solving problems in a country as large as Canada has never been easy. But Canadians have always found peaceful solutions in the past, and no doubt they will continue to do so in the future.

FURTHER INFORMATION

● AIR CANADA
15 W. 50th Street
Rockefeller Center
New York, NY 10020
● CANADIAN HERITAGE
25 Eddy Street, 10th Floor
Hull, Quebec
K1A 0M5
Canada
● CANADIAN TOURIST OFFICE
1251 Avenue of Americas
New York, NY 10020

BOOKS ABOUT CANADA

Alexander, Bryan and Cherry. *Inuit.* Raintree Steck-Vaughn, 1992

Bakken, Edna. *Alberta.* Childrens Press, 1992

MacKay, Kathryn. *Ontario.* Childrens Press, 1992

Malcolm, Andrew H. *The Land and People of Canada.* Harper Collins Books, 1991

Sunday, Jane. *Canada,* "World in View" series. Raintree Steck-Vaughn, 1992

GLOSSARY

CHINOOK
A warm dry wind that blows across the western prairies from the Rockies, causing a rapid rise in the temperature.

CLEAR-CUTTING
A type of forestry where every tree in an area is cut down, leaving the land almost totally bare.

DEFORESTATION
Cutting down large areas of trees, often causing erosion of the land and damage to rivers as soil is washed in to them.

FOSSIL FUELS
Fuels such as coal, oil and natural gas that are formed from the remains of plants and animals that decay underground. The process takes millions of years.

GLACIER
A large mass of ice formed by the build-up of many layers of snow. The pressure of its weight makes it move downhill, very slowly.

MALL
A large building with many shops, businesses, restaurants, and even hotels and recreational facilities, under one roof.

PERMAFROST
Ground that remains frozen all year round. As the top layer thaws in summer, the soil becomes saturated with water, because the ice below prevents water from draining into the ground.

POWWOW
A gathering where native people come together to dance, sing, and socialize.

RESERVE
An area of land set aside for the use of native people. Canada's first reserves were established in 1876.

TUNDRA
Areas of land in the far north where vegetation is limited, because the cold climate means the growing season is short.

INDEX

RUSSIA

Arctic Circle

BERING STRAIT

60°

BEAUFORT
SEA

USA

Holma
Islan

YUKON

NORTHWEST

● Whitehorse

Yellowknife ●

PACIFIC

OCEAN

● Prince Rupert

C

BRITISH
COLUMBIA

Edmonton ●

75°
60°
45°
30°
15°
0°
15°
30°
45°

VANCOUVER
ISLAND

ALBERT

Banff ● Calga

● Vancouver

Lethbridge
Pincher Creek ● ●

Victoria

90° 105° 120° 135° 150° 165° 180° 165° 150° 135° 120° 105° 90° 75° 60° 45° 30° 15° 0° 15° 30° 45° 60° 75° 90°

PROVINCE	AREA sq mi	(sq km)	CAPITAL	POPULATION (1992 estimate)	DATE JOINED CANADIAN CONFEDERATION
Newfoundland	156,649	(405,720)	St John's	581,100	1949
Nova Scotia	21,423	(55,490)	Halifax	920,800	1867
New Brunswick	28,355	(73,440)	Fredericton	749,100	1867
Prince Edward Island	2,185	(5,660)	Charlottetown	130,300	1873
Quebec	594,860	(1,540,660)	Quebec City	7,150,700	1867
Ontario	412,581	(1,068,580)	Toronto	10,609,800	1867
Manitoba	250,947	(649,940)	Winnipeg	1,113,100	1870
Saskatchewan	251,866	(652,330)	Regina	1,004,500	1905
Alberta	255,287	(661,190)	Edmonton	2,632,400	1905
British Columbia	365,900	(947,800)	Victoria	3,451,300	1871
TERRITORY				ESTABLISHED	
Yukon	186,661	(483,450)	Whitehorse	30,200	1898
Northwest Territories	1,322,910	(3,426,320)	Yellowknife	62,300	1870

ARCTIC OCEAN

105°

Cape Columbia

ELLESMERE ISLAND

Eureka

BAFFIN BAY

GREENLAND

BAFFIN ISLAND

VICTORIA ISLAND

LABRADOR SEA

N
E
W
S

TERRITORIES

HUDSON BAY

NEWFOUNDLAND

Twillingate
Gander
St John's

QUEBEC

C A N A D A

MANITOBA

PRINCE EDWARD ISLAND

Cavendish
Charlottetown

NEW BRUNSWICK

ONTARIO

Quebec
Fredericton
Halifax

Saskatoon

SASKATCHEWAN

Regina

Winnipeg

Thunder Bay

Montreal
Hull

NOVA SCOTIA

ATLANTIC OCEAN

OTTAWA

Pickering
Toronto
Hamilton
Fort Erie

U S A

MIDDLE ISLAND

0 ——— 500 mi

1,000 km